Samuel McGavran

A brief history of Harrison county, Ohio

Samuel McGavran

A brief history of Harrison county, Ohio

ISBN/EAN: 9783337125783

Printed in Europe, USA, Canada, Australia, Japan

Cover: Foto ©Andreas Hilbeck / pixelio.de

More available books at **www.hansebooks.com**

S. B. McGarran, M. D.

LAYING OF CORNER STONE NEW COURT HOUSE MAY 17, 1891.

A

BRIEF HISTORY

OF

HARRISON COUNTY, OHIO.

By S. B. McGAVRAN, M. D.

INTRODUCTORY.

-

TO THE PEOPLE OF HARRISON COUNTY:

-

I offer to you a history of your county and mine, and, in doing so, I do not hope to present a perfect picture of the growth and developement of this county from its birth in the wilderness to its present proud position among the rich and enlightened counties of the State of Ohio. I cannot hope to do more than rescue from oblivion and place in readable and consecutive form, such facts that it may contain, and trust that some one in the future may more adequately perform this task.

SAMUEL B. McGAVRAN, M. D.

OUR PIONEERS.

THE laying of the corner-stone of our new court house, this the 17th day of May, 1894, furnishes an auspicious occasion for the study of events which comprise the warp and woof of our civilization and our prosperity. The early inhabitants of the county were from New Jersey, Delaware, Maryland and Pennsylvania. They were men of intelligence, enlightened judgment, iron nerve and indomitable perseverance.

At the time of the organization of our county in 1813 its limits were almost an unbroken wilderness. The wolf, bear and deer roamed at large. The forest was here in all its native majesty and beauty. Here in this wilderness home our pioneer fathers located. Their history might be told in a few words, they built a log cabin—they went to work with ax in hand, prepared to level to the earth the stout monarch of the forest, and make for themselves and families permanent homes, and thereby establish upon a new and virgin soil the securities and blessings of a civilization from which they had been voluntarily divorced. The life of a pioneer was a continued warfare with wild and uncultivated nature. There was no hardship they were not willing to endure, no sacrifices they were not ready to incur. None can tell what has been endured, nor how much expended to convert the deep sounding forests into our present fertile fields. The early settlers of our county were precursors of a mighty race, continually struggling for better conditions, and in their pursuit of lands and wealth and happiness, they sought protection in the establishment of good government — government which should guarantee liberty to all alike in civic affairs, and uniformity of rights in matters of religion. The history of our people is not that of conquests of war, but the victories of peace.

ORGANIZATION OF COUNTY.

The act establishing the county of Harrison passed the legislature January 2d, 1813, to take effect January 1st, 1814. On January 12th the legislature amended the act making it take effect February 1st, 1813. On January 14th, 1813, the legislature passed a resolution appointing three commissioners to locate the county seat for Harrison county. On April 15th, 1813, Jacob Myers, Joseph Richardson and Robert Speer, as commissioners named in the resolution of January 14th, 1813, to locate a seat of justice for Harrison county, made a report to the common pleas court of Jefferson county, fixing Cadiz as the seat of justice for said county.

JAIL.

At a meeting of the commissioners on the 12th of April 1813, they contracted with Joseph Harris for his *Stone Smoke House* for a *Jail*, and employed Charles Chapman to make the necessary repairs. The commissioners at their meeting August 3d, 1813, entered into a contract with George Mires, he being the lowest bidder, to build a wooden jail for the sum of one thousand four hundred and eighty-five dollars. Built of sound oak logs well hewn. September 25th, 1837, the commissioners decided to build a second jail and awarded the contract to Jos. Divine and James

Crossen, for eight thousand two hundred and
forty-nine dollars. March 6th, 1873, the commissioners contracted the building of the third jail for the
sum of $14,674. It was built of stone, slate roof
with eight iron cells. It was a very suitable building. On June 5th, 1893, the roof was entirely destroyed by fire, and the walls more or less damaged.
The stones were sold to the contractor of the new
court house. At this time we have no jail, our pris-
oners are kept in the town lock-up.

FIRST COURTS.

The first courts of Harrison county were held at
the houses of Thos. Stokes and Wm. Grimes. Permanent arrangements were made at a meeting of the
commissioners held April 12, 1813, when they entered into an article of agreement with the trustees of
the Associate Reform Congregation in Cadiz, for the
use of a meeting house belonging to said society for
the term of three years, for the purpose of holding
judicial courts in and for said county. At a meeting
of the commissioners held October 24, 1815, this
article of agreement was renewed with John McFadden and John Jamison, trustees, for the use of the
meeting house for the term of three years, or until
the court house for said county shall be finished. The
first term of court was held in the house of Thomas
Stokes, the 3d day of May, 1813. This was a special
court and not much business transacted. The second term of court was held August 24, 25 and 26.
Judges, Hon. Benjamin Ruggles, President, and
James Roberts, Samuel Boyd and Ephraim Seers,
Esquires, Associate Judges in said county of Harrison. The court appointed Walter B. Beebe prosecuting attorney for the State of Ohio in Harrison
county. The court also ordered that Walter B.
Beebe be allowed the sum of $33.33½ for

his services as prosecutor for the said August term. The following grand jurors appeared: Andrew McNeely, foreman; William Smith, Tachery Baker, William Mercer, William Hamilton, Samuel Gilmore, William Moore, Thomas Hitchcock, John McConnell, William Conwell, Richard McKibben, and John Taggart. On motion of Mr. Beebe, who produced to the court the credentials of William Knox, a minister of the Methodist Episcopal Church, satisfying the court that the said William has been regularly ordained as minister in said church according to the usages thereof, the said William Knox was licensed to solemnize marriages in the State so long as he, the said William, continues a regular minister in said church. The court ordered a license to be granted to John Adams, to keep a tavern at his place of residence in Nottingham township, for one year; also to William Grimes, Mr. Middie, Mr. Niel and Mr. Maholm, to keep a tavern in Cadiz.

The first jury drawn and empanelled were: John Paxton, Samuel Osburn, Jonathan Seers, Robt. Croskey, Samuel Dunlap, James McMillen, Samuel Huff, David Barrett, John Clark, Andrew Richey, James Porter and Benjamin Johnson. The grand jury returned one indictment for larceny, four for riot, and seven for assault and battery.

FIRST COURT HOUSE.

At a meeting of the commissioners July 6, 1815, they gave public notice that on the first Monday of September next, they would offer at public sale the erection of a brick court house, for the use of said county. On the 10th of August, 1815, the commissioners fixed the spot of ground on which the court house for the use of said county is to be built and caused the same to be surveyed off from the public ground in the town of Cadiz. On September 4, 1815 the commissioners exposed at public sale the building of a brick court house, forty-two feet square, which was knocked off to one John McCurdy, he being the lowest bidder, for the sum of five thousand six hundred and ninety-five dollars. This court house was to be finished by the first of April 1819.

On the 24th of July, 1827, the contract was given to John Olmstead to build the county offices, for the sum of $1,299. The bell for the court house was furnished by Daniel Kilgore, June 6, 1829. This court house remained the seat of justice for seventy-four years, and during all this time was used for many purposes other than those of justice. Meetings of all kinds touching the public interests were held within its walls.

County officials of 1813: Auditor, Walter B. Beebe; Treasurer, Samuel Osburn; Clerk of Courts, William Tingley; Prosecuting Attorney, Walter B. Beebe; Sheriff, Elescondo Henderson; County Recorder, William Tingley; Coroner, Charles Chapman; County Commissioners, John Pugh, James Cobean, Eleazer Hoff.

County officials of 1894: Auditor, H. G. Forker; Treasurer, N. E. Clendennin; Clerk of Courts, M. J. McCoy; Prosecuting Attorney, William T. Perry; Sheriff, D. P. Host; County Recorder, Thomas Arbaugh; Coroner, S. H. Kent, D. V. S.; County Commissioners, Thomas Ryder, William C. Adams, John W. Spiker.

SECOND COURT HOUSE.

On the 21st of January, 1893, a meeting was held in the Auditor's office to take action, by which the matter of the erection of a new court house as a necessity to the county should be put in motion. At this meeting Col. John S. Pearce was appointed to prepare a memorial to the legislature, setting forth the need of a new court house. Maj. Cunningham and S. B. McGavran to draft a bill to be submitted to the legislature, for its approval, authorizing the county commissioners to issue bonds in the amount not exceeding $100,000 with which to build a new court house in Cadiz. The memorial and bill were duly forwarded to our Representative, Hon. R. G. Kean. The following is the copy of the memorial as prepared by Col. Pearce:

TO THE GENERAL ASSEMBLY OF OHIO:

We, the undersigned citizens of Harrison county, do hereby respectfully petition your honorable body to enact a law authorizing and requiring the commissioners of said county, to build a new court house at Cadiz, the present county seat, of sufficient size to contain suitable rooms for the holding of the several courts for said county, including that of the probate court and all the county offices, not to exceed, however, in price, the sum of one hundred thousand dollars, and we state the following reasons therefor:

First: The present court house and the other county buildings which are outside of it, are all old and in a dilapidated condition, having been built in the year 1816, and are now too small and crowded for the proper and safe keeping of their records and office papers, and the convenient transaction of business therein, and especially have they become very unsafe places for the keeping of such records and papers. The court house is so constructed that it is almost impossible, especially during sessions of the grand jury, to hold court therein, on account of the confusion created thereby, the grand jury and its witnesses having no other means of access to the jury room than by a stairway in said court room and owing to the construction of the building this cannot be remedied, and has always existed.

Second: The office of the Probate Judge is in the rooms over the fire engine house, formerly the old market house, and is (if possible) in a worse condition for the want of capacity, and convenience for the transaction of its business and safety of its records, than any of the other offices. This room is not only a very unsafe place, for the records and papers of such office, the destruction of which, by fire, would cost the county more than would the building of a new court house, but it is also difficult and dangerous of access, especially so, for aged and infirm persons. The truth is, not one of the county buildings is a safe place for the keeping of its records and office papers, the destruction of which in any of them, by fire, would be an irreparable and incalculable loss to the county.

Third: A new court house containing all the county offices and court rooms, would not only be a great convenience to those having business to transact with them, but would be economy in the end in the expenditure of the public money, in providing places of safety for the public records and papers, and convenient transaction of business therein.

The foregoing are some of the facts upon which we base this application for a new court house, others might be given, but we deem it unnecessary to do so; those given being sufficient in our judgment to justify this petition and its prayers. Should there be any question made as to the correctness of the above statements of facts we would respectfully ask that your honorable body appoint a suitable committee to make a personal examination of them for itself.

The following is the copy of the bill as prepared by Major Cunningham:

Section 1. Be it enacted by the General Assembly of the State of Ohio: That the commissioners of Harrison county, Ohio, are hereby authorized and required to construct, without unnecessary delay, a court house on the public square at the county seat of said county, at a cost not to exceed one hundred thousand dollars. For the construction of such building, bids are to be received as provided by law: but no bid shall be entertained by said commissioners that shall exceed the sum of one hundred thousand dollars as herein authorized for the completion of the entire building.

Section 2. That the county commissioners of said county, for the purpose of constructing said court house, are hereby authorized to borrow such sums of money as may be necessary, at a rate not exceeding six per cent. per annum, and issue the bonds of said county to secure the payment of principal and interest thereon; such interest shall be paid semi-annually at the office of the county treasurer. Said bonds shall be issued and sold in all respects in pursuance of existing law at not less than their face value, and the principal shall be paid at the said county treasurer's office at such times as the commissioners shall prescribe, not exceeding nine years after date, and said bonds shall specify the object for which they were issued. The commissioners shall, annually, at their June session, levy such amount of taxes as will fully meet the interest on such indebtedness and at least one-ninth of the principal.

Section 3. This act shall take effect and be in force from and after its passage.

The bill was introduced in the House of Representatives January 27th by Hon. R. G. Kean, and read the second time January 30th, and referred to the committee on county affairs. Mr. Kean announced that the bill would not be hurried through, but that sufficient time would be given to discuss the claims for the new court house as set up in the memorial of Col. Pearce. The opposition to the bill became so formidable that the committee of county affairs came to Cadiz on Friday, the 17th day of February, 1893. After the committee in this manner investigated the necessity for a new court house for themselves, they reported favorable, and the bill passed the House February 28, 1893, without a dissenting vote.

A like committee of the Senate visited Cadiz, March 17, 1893, and after a complete examination of our *old* buildings and hearing arguments on both sides, the bill was recommended favorably and passed March 22, 1893.

A supplementary act passed the House April 13, 1893, authorizing the Judge of Common Pleas Court to appoint a building committee. The Court appointed David Cunningham, William H. Arnold, A. O. Barnes and W. A. Holmes.

The building committee, with the county commissioners, W. C. Adams, Thos. H. Ryder and John W. Spiker, employed Yost and Packard, of Columbus, Ohio, as architects. The plans and specifications were carefully prepared, and the building of the court house was awarded to E. M. Long, of Bowerston, August 12, 1893, the contract price being $86,985.

THE DESCRIPTION OF THE NEW COURT HOUSE.

The building will be in round numbers 100 feet square. No. 1 Berea stone for body and Oolitic lime stone for trimmings. The Berea stone comes from the Cleveland Stone Company, of Cleveland, Ohio.

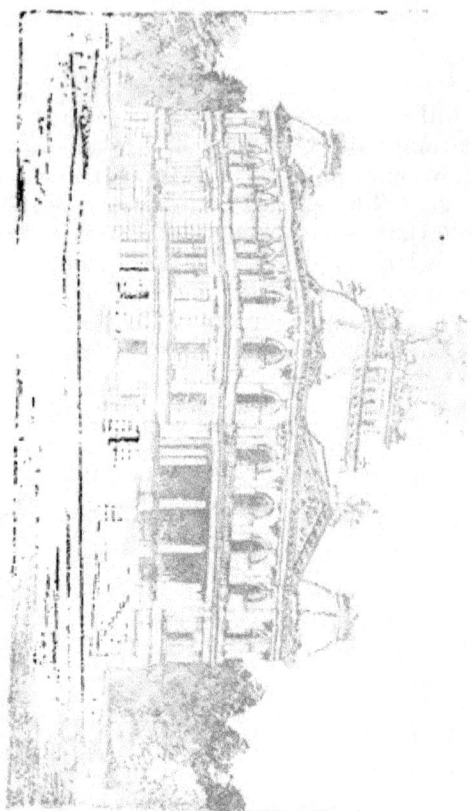

The lime stone from the Oolite Quarry Company, of Spencer, Indiana. The basement, which is all above the grade line, will contain a large public hall, with a committee room attached; two large rooms suitable for the post-office or the public library; one large office, lavatory, heating room, fuel room, etc.; the Smead system of dry closets; wide windows, tile floors, making every part of basement easy of access. On the first floor will be found the Auditor's office, with book room, and a door opening into the Commissioner's office. Opposite the Auditor's office will be the Treasurer's office and the Surveyor's office. In the rear of the first floor will be found the Recorder's office, the Probate Court and the Prosecuting Attorney's office. Wide corridors leading to the rotunda, make every part of the floor easy of access.

The floors in the corridors and outside the railings, will be of tile, all other floors of oak laid on concrete.

On the second floor there will be the Court Room, with the ceiling of ornamented leaded glass, with a sky-light above, guaranteeing a good light and a pleasant room. In connection, and conveniently located, will be rooms for male and female witnesses, the Judge's room, offices of the Clerk and Sheriff, Grand Jury room, Petit Jury room, and Library.

The building will be heated by hot water, wired for electric lights, and plumbed for gas and water.

The entire building will be made as near fire-proof as possible. All the floors, beams, ceilings, and roof construction will be of iron. A tower 112 feet high will ornament the building, in which will be a town clock and on it a figure of Justice.

The following are the names of the Presiding and Associate Judges in Harrison county up to 1852:

PRESIDENTS.

Benjamin Ruggles, Geo. W. Belden, Wm. Kennon, Benj. S. Cowan.

ASSOCIATE JUDGES.

James Roberts, Samuel Boyd, Ephraim Sears, Matthew Simpson, Alex. Henderson, John McCullough, John McCurdy, Thomas Bingham, David Campbell, John McBean, Robert Maxwell, Joseph Hunter, Alexander Patterson, John Hanna, Samuel Moorehead, Thomas Lee, Jas. Maxwell, Wm. McFarland, Wm. Boggs.

I herewith submit a complete list of the county officials and members of the State Legislature from the organization of the county down to the present time.

STATE SENATORS.

John McLaughlin John Dunlap, Samuel G. Berryhill, *Matthew Simpson,*[*] James Roberts, *Daniel Kilgore, Joseph Holmes,* Thomas C. Vincent, John Brady, *Chauncey Dewey,* Robert H. Miller, John Hastings, Pinckney Lewis, *Samuel G. Peppard,* David Allen, *Charles Warfel,* Isaac Holloway, *Marshall McCall,* Isaac Welch, *John C. Jamison,* Henry West, *James B. Jamison, Sam'l Knox,* David Wagener, *D. A. Hollingsworth,* Solomon Hogue, *George W. Glover,* Chas. N. Snyder, J. W. Nichols, *Charles M. Hogg.*

REPRESENTATIVES.

Stephen Ford, Robt. Patterson, Andrew McNeely, James Willson, Thomas Elliott, James Moores, William Moore, John Patterson, Ephraim Sears, William Willy, Walter B. Beebe, Joseph Rea, Saml. W. Bostwick, John Gruber, Josiah Scott, William McFarland, Jacob Lemmon, Samuel A. Russell, Wm.

[*] Were residents of the County.

16   *A Brief History*

Hammond, Marshall McCall, Reynolds K. Price,
Ephraim Clark, James Day, William H. McGavran,
John Latham, Smith R. Watson, Ingram Clark,
Lewis Lewton, Anderson P. Lacey, David Cun-
ningham, Samuel Herron, A. C. Nixon, Jesse For-
sythe, Oliver G. Cope, Samuel B. McGavran, Jas-
per N. Lantz, Geo. M. Patton, Wesley B. Hearn,
Robert G. Kean, Samuel K. McLaughlin.

PROBATE JUDGES.

Brice W. Viers, Allen C. Turner, Amon Lemmon,
E. B. McNamee.

AUDITORS.

The first Auditor (or Clerk of the Commissioners
as the office was then called) was Walter B. Beebe,
who held the position until Nov. 4, 1816, and Lared
Stinson was appointed, and after that J. S. Hanna.
Subsequently the Auditors have been:

Joseph Herris, Joseph Meek, James Miller, Chas.
Patterson, Z. Bayless, J. Sharp, R. Edney, R. K.
Price, John Sloan, Wm. S. Gramfell, S. W. Kinsey,
Samuel Knox, W. H. McCoy, R. A. McCormick,
W. O. Potts, T. W. Giles, J. M. Scott, Henry
Spence, Geo. A. Crew, H. G. Forker.

TREASURERS.

Samuel Osburn, J. S. Lacey, Samuel McCormick,
James McNutt, Wm. Milligan, Zephemiah Bayless,
Ralph Barcroft, David Hilbert, John Russell, Thos.
Richey, Frank Grace, W. S. Poulson, Elias Foust,
Geo. A. Haverfield, H. L. Thompson, N. B. Pumph-
rey, A. J. Harrison, S. A. Moore, N. E. Clendennin,
Robert Stewart.

PROSECUTING ATTORNEYS.

Walter B. Beebe, Josiah Scott, Edwin M. Stanton,
S. W. Bostwick, Thos. L. Jewett, S. G. Peppard,

A. C. Turner, Lewis Lewton, Jesse H. McMath, Amon Lemmon, W. P. Hayes, David Cunningham, John S. Pearce, D. A. Hollingsworth, John C. Given, John M. Garvin, Walter G. Shotwell, William T. Perry.

COUNTY CLERKS.

William Tingley, Thomas C. Vincent, Samuel M. McCormick, Chas. Patterson, T. C. Rowels, R. M. Lyons, John Fogle, J. M. Garvin, A. W. Scott, E. B. McNamee, M. J. McCoy, E. B. Kirby.

COUNTY RECORDERS.

William Tingley, I. Harris, Wm. Johnson, S. M. McCormick, M. M. Sloan, Wm. Boyce, Lancelot Hearn, Wm. A. Hern, Joseph Rea, Geo. Woodburn, John Graybill, L. B. Grimes, A. B. Hines, Thomas Arbaugh.

SHERIFFS.

Elescondo Henderson, James Boswell, John Stokes, Rezin Arnold, Barrick Dickerson, John S. Lacey, Matthew McCoy, James McNut, William Milligan, William Cady, William Barrett, David Hilbert, Jas. Boyd, Alex. Barger, E. S. Woodburn, S. K. McGee, J. E. McPeck, James Moore, S. S. Hamill, Elisha Hargrave, E. Howard, J. C. Carver, J. C. Glover, A. Quigley, D. P. Host.

COMMISSIONERS.

John Pugh, James Cobean, Eleazer Huff; Wm. Wiley, Wm. Phillips, John Craig, Robert Maxwell, Wm. Henderson, Joseph Holmes, David Thompson, Thos. Martin, Brice W. Viers, John Caldwell, Henry Ford, John Ramage, Samuel Colvin, Jesse Merrill, John Sharp, Andrew Richey, James P. Beall, Thomas Day, John Downing, James Hogland, Samuel Hitchcock, Samuel Richey, Luther Rowley, John Carrick, John Yost, Elijah Carver, Joseph Masters,

Jacob Cramlet, Jackson Croskey, Chas. Wells, Jas. J. Billingsley. Walter Craig, Andrew Jamison, Levi Snyder, Wm. Evans, James Patton, John Sloan, Alex. Henderson, John Latham, Thos. McMillen, E. W. Phillips, Geo. Love, L. M. Branson, Jackson Rea, John Miller, M. B. Fierbaugh, R. B. Moore, Andrew Smith, John W. Spiker, Wm. C. Adams, Thos. H. Ryder.

Harrison county has furnished two Congressman, Daniel Kilgore and John A. Bingham. Two members of the Board of Equalization, Walter Jamison, and C. A. Skinner. Members of Constitutional Conventions, 1850 1851, Samuel Moorehead; 1872—1873, William G. Waddle.

The Cadiz bar has been honored by men of talent among the most prominent of whom were: Walter

OLD COURT HOUSE. BUILT IN 1816; TORN DOWN AUGUST 1883.

B. Beebe, Edwin M. Stanton, Chauncey Dewey, Stewart B. Shotwell, Samuel W. Bostwick, Samuel A. Russell, Josiah Scott, Joseph Sharon, Jesse H. McMath, Lewis Lewton, J. M. Estep.

At this time, May 10, 1894, the following attorneys are actively engaged in practicing in Cadiz:— David Cunningham, John S. Pearce, Amon Lemmon, David A. Hollingsworth, John M. Garvin, Walter G. Shotwell, A. O. Barnes, Milton Taggart, James Moore, John Busby, W. T. Perry, J. B. Worley, P. W. Boggs.

Surveyor in 1813, Hugh Shotwell. Surveyor in 1894, Jacob Jarvis.

INFIRMARIES.

THE FIRST INFIRMARY.

At a special meeting of the commissioners April 23, 1825, they made a contract with Samuel Boyd for 104 acres of land, (this farm is now owned by Norwood and Samuel Hedges,) for a poor farm for said county, and there being a house thereon, the commissioners appointed Walter B. Beebe, Thomas Lewis, Jacob Webb, Michael Moore, Joseph Johnson, John Hurless, John Patterson, and Matthew Simpson, directors of the poor establishment in our said county. March 20, 1826, the directors of the poor reported that they had taken possession of the poor house and appointed John Willson as superintendent.

Number of inmates—males 3, females 1.

Paid Supt. for keeping poor and clothing same $162.17.

Paid Supt. for making rails $6.00.
Paid Supt. for making stakes, $1.00.
To Samuel Lewis for support of outdoor poor $12.
To Dr. W. R. Slemmons medical attendance, $4.00.
To Walter B. Beebe, blank book, $2.00.

SECOND INFIRMARY.

On the 3d day of April, 1832, the commissioners, Thomas Martin, David Thompson and John Caldwell, contracted with Sheridan Cox for 303 acres of land in Archer township for $3636, for the poor farm. The commissioners gave Robert Watson $240.85 for building a poor house on this farm. This farm was sold to Matthew McCoy. George Cox, superintendent.

THIRD INFIRMARY.

On the 1st day of April, 1835, Henry Ford, John Ramage and Samuel Colvine, commissioners, bought from Walter McClintock, 60 acres of land, also in Archer township for $450 for a poor house farm. This farm is now owned by Benjamin Reed. The directors of the poor house at this time were Edmund Tipton, Daniel Welch and William Arnold. This farm was sold August 1, 1845, to Samuel Pittenger and Abraham Busby. Supt. at this time Wm. Speer. Number of inmates 9.

FOURTH INFIRMARY.

The commissioners on the 6th of June, 1845, purchased from Nathaniel McFadden, 124 acres of land for an infirmary, situated on the State road leading from Cadiz to New Philadelphia, for the sum of $4000. On the 6th of August, 1845, the commissioners entered into an article of agreement with Thomas McCreary and Henry Boyles as principal, and William Tingley, John Olmstead and Chauncey

Dewey as securities, for the building of the poor house. The building was 74 feet long and 40 feet wide, built of brick, two stories high, for the sum of $3740.

This building remained in use until 1884, when the question of building a new infirmary was submitted to a vote of the people, and carried by a large majority. A new building was therefore erected in 1884 5. It is a handsome structure, three stories high. The basement of stone, the balance brick; contains 91 rooms, and is heated by hot air. The official report, ending September, 1893, shows the the number of inmates 48. The infirmary farm contains about 400 acres. Welch Rogers was appointed superintendent April 1, 1894. In this institution the benevolent spirit of the county finds its noblest expression.

INFIRMARY DIRECTORS.

Walter B. Beebe,
Thomas Lewis,
Matthew Simpson,
Michael Moore,
Joseph Johnson,
John Hurless,
John Patterson,
Jacob Webb,
Chauncey Dewey,
Matthew McCoy,
Thomas Wilson,
Thomas Taylor,
George Cox,
Samuel W. Bostwick,
John Prichard,
William Henderson,
John Patterson,
Josiah Scott,
Daniel Welsh,
Edmund Tipton,
Robert H. Miller,
Wm. Arnold,
Wm. Smiley,
Jacob Rheam,
David Finnicum,
Jacob Hostman,
Daniel McBrevy,
Henry Maxwell,
Samuel McCormick,
Joseph McCullough,
Jacob Hines,
Abraham Busby.

John Welch,
James Lee,
Robert Orr,
Josiah Crawford,
Robert Givin,
John Haverfield,
Samuel Moorehead,
Hugh Nellravy,
John Conaway,
John Rogers,
Samuel Adams,
John C. Barger,
Alexander Haverfield,
John Lisle,
John Osborn,
John N. Haverfield,
Wm. Spiker,
Henry Fisher,
Geo. Heberlin,
James N. Adams,
J. G. Kennedy,
John Roley,
Samuel Dickerson,
James J. Billingsley,
L. A. Lawrence,
S. W. Adams,
John McDivitt,
John Beadle,
John Barclay,
James M. Hines,
John N. Hanes.

CHILDREN'S HOME.

The Harrison County Children's Home is located in the eastern part of the county, one mile southeast of the corporate limits of Cadiz.

The farm consists of twenty-five acres, with two springs of water on it, and is perhaps one of the most favorable situations in the county.

The Home is on the Cottage plan.

The buildings, except the barn, are brick, and were all made on the grounds, facing brick were hand-pressed.

The main building, 80x46 feet, is two stories high above a nine foot basement, and has an eight foot finished attic. It has twenty-three rooms, and all are amply large for their several requirements.

The Cottage fronts the pike but stands back fifty feet, is 80x26 feet, two stories. First floor contains boys' and girls' play rooms, with Cottage Matron's room in center. On the second floor are the dormitories and wardrobes. These rooms can easily be flooded with sunlight and air, which makes them very healthy for sleeping in.

The heating is all done by grates and hall stoves.

The water supply is good, having two cisterns with capacity of five hundred barrels and put into the large steel tanks up in the buildings by wind power.

The following is the report of the visiting committee for the year ending August 23, 1893:

TO HIS HONOR, JUDGE MANSFIELD:

There are at this date in the Home 36 inmates. Males 23, females 13. Received since last report 31; indentured 10; returned to parents 8; transferred 2. We take pleasure in noting the condition of this institution. The buildings are large, nicely and healthfully arranged, and most beautifully located. Economy, neatness, discipline and order characterize its management by its present very efficient superintendent.

Great care is being taken in preparing good homes for the children. We are satisfied there are other children in our county who ought to receive the benefit to be derived from so efficient a home as this is, and are led to believe the fault lies at the door of the township trustees.

We find at the Home a good daily school under the supervision of a competent teacher, and confidently believe that many will go out from this institution both intellectually and morally, fully able to cope with the many who have been more highly favored. The institution as conducted is certainly a very great blessing to these poor unfortunates who come within its influence. Respectfully submitted,

WILLIAM CROSKEY,
JUDITH JOHNSON,
MARGARET McCREADY,
D. B. WELCH,
Committee.

Superintendent, Capt. Andrew Smith. Trustees of the Home, Hon. James B. Jamison, L. M. Branson, M. B. Fierbaugh and Edward Clifford.

CHURCHES.

Our forefathers were not forgetful of their higher christian duties. In many instances with the smoke that curled in currents from the chimneys of their log cabins ascended the incense of prayer. The rude primeval hut, instead of being the abode of the little family cluster alone, became a temple of worship. Our first churches—Dr. Crawford in his historical address, says that the Rankin Methodist church was organized in David Rankin's log cabin 1814. It is said the first prayer meeting held in this county was at Buskirk's log cabin and from it arose the Dickerson Methodist church. The first sermon ever preached in Cadiz was by the Rev. John Rea, Presbyterian minister 1804, at the base of a large walnut tree that stood south of the court house site.

We have in Harrison county according to the census report of Samuel G. Peppard for the year ending 1890, twelve distinct religious denominations.

The number of Sabbath School scholars, communicants enrolled, also valuation and seating capacity are as follows:

CHURCHES.	S. S. S.	MEMBERS.	VALUE.	SEATS.
Friends..........3	95	383	$ 3,800	815
A. M. E. Church..2	42	160	3,000	500
United Brethren5	300	442	7,720	1,760
Presbyterian 13	1178	1747	55,500	4,950
United Pres...... 6	369	507	28,500	2,200
Adventists........ 1		14	500	120
Meth. Protesta't.1		60	300	400
German Reform.1	132	62	1,500	400
Meth. Episcopal34	3332	3335	89,600	10,850
Lutheran 2	150	181	4,000	550
Baptist 3	209	100	2,250	500
Disciples..........4	213	244	3,750	1,250
Union S.S.'s....13	550			

Thus it will be seen we have in the county 90 places of public worship; number of Sunday school scholars 6,570 and 7,133 church members. The total value of church property is $200,820, with a seating capacity for 24,235 persons, enough to seat every man, woman and child in the county. Value of parsonages $21,000.

SCHOOLS AND COLLEGES.

We trust we will not be considered as dealing in extravagant assertions when we say that the cause of education in Harrison county is perhaps as far advanced as any other county in the State, and that in its progress and development, it can challenge comparison with the foremost in Ohio. The first settlers did not neglect or overlook its vital claims, and the subscription school was early encouraged and put to practical working, and answered a noble and sublime purpose in those dim by-gone days.

There are at present 9 special school districts, 97 sub-districts. In each of these districts we have good school houses and the best of teachers. We have from six to nine months of school each year. It costs about $70,000 a year to run our schools.

SCIO COLLEGE.

Scio College was chartered in 1866. It has had about 600 graduates. It belongs to the Methodist Episcopal Church.

The College comprises seven district departments, each complete within itself: Collegiate, Pharmacy, Music, Business, Elocution, Art, Shorthand and Typewriting.

The Literary course comprises a three years' preparatory and a four years' collegiate course, making seven years in all, and ranks in this respect with the very best schools in the State. The Music course comprises four years' work; the Pharmacy, two terms of six months each.

The total enrollment of different students last year was 548, from ten different States and countries.

The Faculty is at present composed of fifteen teachers. In the point of numbers the College ranks about sixth among the Colleges and Universities of this State; in comprehensiveness and thoroughness, we are among the first. Two large buildings are devoted to school work, using over 30,000 feet of floor space.

FRANKLIN COLLEGE.

This College is located in the village of New Athens, was chartered January 22, 1825, and formally opened June 8, 1825, with Rev. William McMillan, of Canonsburg, Pa., as President, and John Armstrong, of Pittsburgh, Pa., as Professor of Mathematics.

Since its opening this institution has sent out over five hundred graduates; ninety per cent. of whom have entered some of the learned professions and sixty per cent. of whom have entered the ministry.

In 1840, owing to the decided anti-slavery charac-

SCIO COLLEGE, SCIO, HARRISON COUNTY, O.

ter of the College a pro-slavery rival was established in the same village under the name of Providence
College, but this was soon abandoned for want of
sufficient patronage, and the original College has
been allowed to run an uninterrupted course down to
the present time, when we still find it in a most
flourishing condition.

HOPEDALE NORMAL COLLEGE.

The College at Hopedale, first known as "The
McNeely Normal School" and later, after assuming
the power to grant degrees, as "Hopedale Normal
College" nas been a power in the land. Its proprietor, Cyrus McNeely, aspired, in its establishment,
not so much to educate *at the top* as to educate well
at the bottom.

Hopedale was the first college in Eastern Ohio

HOPEDALE NORMAL COLLEGE.

which opened its doors for the co-education of the
sexes.

"Old Franklin" had for many years been making
professional men: it was left to Hopedale to make

teachers for the common schools and fit men for the duties of non-professional life.

Its first start was as a school with three departments, the highest under the management of Dr. York, a practicing physician of the village and a graduate of "Franklin." Then followed at the helm Edwin Regal, John Ogden, Wm. Brinkerhoff and Dr. Jamieson.

In all the leading cities of the country are men who owe their success to training at Hopedale. Prof. Brinkerhoff was the pioneer stenographer of this region, and his students were enabled by his instruction, to make this a stepping stone to higher achievements.

Over 7000 students have been enrolled upon the College books, and the work which its originator has accomplished can never be fully known "until the leaves of the judgment book unfold."

HARRISON COUNTY IN THE WAR OF THE REBELLION.

WASHINGTON CITY, April 13, 1861.

MESSRS. HATTON & ROWLES,

EDITORS CADIZ REPUBLICAN: Fort Sumpter has been battered down by the traitor hoards of the South. It is the first battle upon this continent and of this century waged in defense of chattel slavery, the worst despotism which ever cursed the earth or disgraced and outraged humanity. I repeat now what I

said in my place as your Representative last January,
—the question of to-day is not whether the constitution of our country shall be amended, but whether
the constitution shall be maintained. Upon the solu-
tion of this question depends the fate of the Repub-
lic. President Lincoln thus far "clear in his great
office," will, I trust, soon summon the loyal citizens
of every section to come to the rescue of a violated
constitution, let them come as the winds come, when
forests are rending; let them come as the waves come,
when the navies are stranding. May God defend the
right.   Truly yours,
                    JOHN A. BINGHAM.

A rousing war meeting was held in the court house
on the evening of April 20, 1861, to raise a company
of volunteers in response to a call of President Lincoln for 75,000 men to suppress the Rebellion. The
war feeling was up to fever heat, and the enthusiasm
intense. The court house was filled to overflowing
and many were unable to get seats. Hon. John A.
Bingham addressed the meeting for about an hour in
a strain of melting eloquence which stirred the aud-
ience as a tornado stirs the forest. The old cannon
which had long been given over to rust was drawn
from the hiding place and awoke the surrounding
hills with its thundering tones. The soul stirring
fife and rattling drum aroused the enthusiasm of
young America. Flags were floating all over town.
A fund of several thousand dollars was raised to
support the families of those who enlisted in their
country's service.

The excitement kept up at fever heat, every thing
was War, WAR, WAR! Meetings were held all
over the county, and in less than a week more than
one hundred volunteered. Cadiz on Monday morn-
ing, April 22d, presented quite a military appear-

ance. The volunteer company was being drilled by General Warfel. Crowds were upon the streets and upon the corners, gathering in squads talking war. I give below the names of the first company from Harrison county:

John Castill, captain; John Conwell, first lieutenant; Miles J. Saunders, second lieutenant; John C. Bayless, Benjamin Turner, John C. Burns, Harris Hatton, Edward W. Kittering, William Randall, Thomas C. Rea, Thomas C. McIlravy, Zenos Poulson, Edward B. Young, William P. Rea, James M. Crawford, John Castill, James A. Laizure, William H. Matlock, David Lowmiller, William Scott, Edward Harner, James Tipton, John Bryan, William H. Bryan, Melvin H. Hearn, Thomas Giles, Franklin K. Mealy, John Clifford, John K. Hatton, Charley A. Leslie, R. Hamilton Kildow, Samuel McMillen, John Anderson, Benjamin Cooper, William McIntire, Vincent S. Boggs, Charles Rawlson, James Saylor, William Morgan, David Murdock, William H. Wheeler, Joseph Ferrell, John J. Jones, William R. Pugh, George W. Bricker, John Kimmel, Hugh R. McGowan, Eli Shields, Isaac Harris, John C. McRea, William P. Shisler, David D. Hoover, Harvey B. Right, John T. Boals, Isaac W. Liggett, Thomas Moody, Joseph G. Moody, William Crogun, Samuel C. Miller, William T. Ramsey, James H. Stewart, George C. Finney, James Crumley, John Martin, James Rittenhouse, John Watters, Jasper Denning, Benjamin T. Anderson, John Handy, Robert Peacock, Samuel B. Adkins, William V. B. Croskey, Alexander Miller, Emanuel Howard, Robert Moore, Salmon Murphy, John A. Tier, John McConkey, Henry J. McFadden, William J. Holloway, John Locke, John G. Kennedy, William H. H. Mills, Jonathan R. Laizure, Festus Jones, John M.

FRANKLIN COLLÆGE, NEW ATHENS, O.

Thompson, John B. Martin, James D. Smith, William Baldwin, William A. Nicolas, George Welling, James Mahollin, William Jones, Samuel Mull, Levi Peddycourt, Nathan H. Baker, James W. Watson, Daniel Holloway, D. N. Fowler, Nelson Driggs, Joshua Lowdon, John W. Butterfield, David Hilligas, Sanford Timmons.

This company left for Columbus on Saturday, April 27, 1861. Their departure was witnessed by two or three thousand persons, every one of whom seemed to be impressed with the solemnity of the occasion. Amidst the cheers of the crowd the boys embarked for the war.

Tears coursed down manly cheeks, and among the women there was scarcely a dry eye. A copy of the New Testament was presented to each of the volunteers at the close of a very solemn and impressive prayer meeting held for their benefit at the court house on the Saturday evening previous to their departure for Camp Jackson, Columbus. Each man was also presented with a beautiful pin-cushion and needle-case composed of the red, white and blue. We regret that we cannot go into detail as to other companies from this county. Harrison county did her full share from the beginning to the end of the war.

We were represented in the 13th Regiment O. V. I. 105; 30th Regiment O. V. I. 123; 43d Regiment O. V. I. 182; 74th Regiment O. V. I. 154; 5th O. V. I. 25; 12th Cavalry 50; 98th Regiment O. V. I. 204; 126th Regiment O. V. I. 371; 69th Regiment O. V. I. 140; 170th Regiment O. V. I. 420; 180th Regiment O. V. I. 30; 11th Cavalry 30. Total 1924. Some in other Regiments 80th, 51st, and W. Va. Cavalry; enough in other regiments to make two thousand soldiers from Harrison county.

HARRISON COUNTY BANKS AND BANKERS.

THE HARRISON NATIONAL BANK.

"Among the many contemporaneous institutions of financial and fiduciary character in this county, the Harrison National Bank, of Cadiz, maintains a position of undoubted consideration."

It is the legitimate descendant from the Harrison branch of the State Bank of Ohio, which was founded in 1841. It was re-organized as a National Bank in accordance with the requirements of the National Banking system in 1865, and re-chartered in 1885. Its capital stock at the present time $100,000, surplus fund $110,000.

The officers of this bank are well-known professional business men and capitalists, consisting of David Cunningham, President, J. M. Sharon, Cashier, A. P. Sheriff, Teller, Miss Emma Wortman and Ralph Cunningham book-keepers. The directors are James Porter, D. Cunningham, L. M. Branson, H. S. Barricklow, John C. Jamison, Dr. J. S. McBean, James Bullock and J. M. Sharon.

THE FIRST NATIONAL BANK.

The First National Bank, of Cadiz, is a reliable and efficiently managed institution. It was reorganized under the National Banking Laws in 1863 as No. 100 with a capital stock of $120,000.

The officers of this bank are D. B. Welch, President, Walter Craig, Vice-President, I. C. Moore,

THE HARRISON NATIONAL BANK, CADIZ.

Cashier, W. S. Cessna, Assistant Cashier, Walter Potts, Book-keeper. The board of directors are D. B. Welch, Walter Craig, William Fox, William Henderson, L. A. Welch, R. W. Barricklow, Samuel Knox, W. B. Beebe Jr.

THE FARMERS AND MECHANICS NATIONAL BANK.

The Farmers and Mechanics National Bank, of Cadiz, is a solid and reliable institution. Was duly organized May 11th, 1874, and incorporated as a National Bank in January, 1878, with a capital stock of $50,000. Surplus of $27,500. The officers of the bank are Melford J. Brown, President, C. O. F. Brown, cashier, Miss Alice Carnahan, Book-keeper. The board of directors consists of Wm. L. Houser, John N. Haverfield, C. O. F. Brown, John M. Garvin, C. A. Skinner, C. M. Hogg and Melford Brown.

THE FOURTH NATIONAL BANK.

The Fourth National Bank, of Cadiz, the youngest of our financial institutions, commenced business March 28th, 1893, with a capital stock paid up of $120,000. Its stock-holders number 250 persons, living in Harrison and adjoining counties. Its President is Samuel Thompson, John E. McPeck, Vice-President. J. M. Schreiber, Cashier, C. E. Stewart, Teller. Board of directors, J. S. Black, David Allison, John E. Kyser, Henry Barricklow, J. W. Clendenning, Dr. W. T. Sharp, J. C. Dysart, T. E. Johnson, Joseph Starr, M. N. Giffin, Milton Taggart, John E. McPeck, Samuel Thompson and Dr. S. B. McGavran.

BANK OF FREEPORT.

The Bank of Freeport was established by Thos. Green in 1893 as a private bank. In 1894 a co-partnership was formed consisting of Thomas Green, John M. Garvin and J. M. Schreiber. The bank enjoys the confidence of the people.

BANK OF SCIO.

The Bank of Scio was organized in July, 1883, by
B. S. Hogue and William Donaldson. This bank is
well-managed, and has contributed in no small de-
gree to the business interests of Scio and vicinity.

ROADS.

The making of roads has been from early times,
one of the most important subjects that has occupied
the attention of the commissioners and tax payers.
Many petitions were presented to the county commissioners during the year 1813, asking for new roads,
all of which seem to have been granted. Thence-
forth for many years they were kept busy providing
for new roads and making changes in old ones.
Road-making in a hilly region is laborious and ex-
pensive, and while we have at this time roads in every
direction, it is still an open question how to make
better ones. We have a pike from Cadiz to New
Athens, Cadiz to Harrisville, Cadiz to Unionvale,
and all the roads leading from Cadiz have from one-
half to two miles of pike.

RAILROADS.

Harrison county has three railroads passing
through it: The P. C. C. & St. L. R. R. and siding 34.98 miles. The P. C. C. & St. L. R. R. second track 23.42 miles. The P. C. C. & St. L. R.
R., Cadiz branch 7.85 miles. C. L. & W. R. R. and
siding 17.64 miles. W. & L. E. R. R. and siding,
27.81 miles. Total number of miles 111.70. Total
valuation $1,324,140.

NEWSPAPERS.

The first newspaper published in Harrison county was in 1816, called the *Cadiz Informant*, afterward called the *Harrison Telegraph*, and the name *Cadiz Republican* given to it in 1840 by Wm. R. Allison. *The Cadiz Republican*, W. B. Hearn, editor and proprietor, therefore lays claim to being the oldest newspaper in the county. *The Cadiz Sentinel*, W. H. Arnold, editor, is the next oldest paper in the county, having been established in 1832.

Other papers in the county are *The Harrison Tribune*, A. B. Lacey editor and proprietor, Cadiz, Ohio. *Harrison County Democrat*, A. N. McCombs editor, and published by the Harrison County Democrat Publishing Company. *The Freeport Press*, McMath & Williams, proprietors, L. B. Williams, editor. *The Scio Herald*, Scio, edited and owned by R. M. Dewey. *Jewett Age*, Jewett, O. A. Hare, owner. *New Athens Review*, published by T. B. Williams, at New Athens.

HARRISON COUNTY AGRICULTURAL SOCIETY.

On June 5, 1834, the county commissioners under provision of law, directed a call to be published in *The Cadiz Sentinel*, looking to the formation of an Agricultural Society, but nothing effective was done under that call, or in any other way until 1846. The matter was then taken up by some of the progressive farmers, chiefly in the eastern part of the county.

The first fair was held in Georgetown in 1846. After that in Cadiz. For the next six years the stock was shown on the streets or in Dewey's field, now Lincoln Avenue, or in Walter Jamison's field, or some other convenient place. Agricultural implements, farm products and domestic goods, were shown in the court house or some of the churches. A plowing match was held each year.

It was not until 1853 that the Society had a permanent location; they then secured Sharp's grove, near town, (now Porter's) and four or five acres were enclosed with a strong, substantial fence, and suitable buildings were erected. The fair was held Oct. 10 and 11, 1853. It was the largest and best attended of any that had taken place. The crowd was estimated at 10,000. There was a large entry of sheep and horses. The floral hall was very attractive, the ladies taking great interest in it. One of the most attractive and exciting features of the fair was a contest of horse-back riding by ladies. Competitors for the premium were: Miss Norton, of St. Clairsville, Mrs. Obediah Slemmons, Miss Amanda Simeral, Miss Gilmore, Miss Shotwell, Miss Taggart, of Cadiz, and Miss Caroline Kennedy, of Green township. All were expert riders and evinced a graceful style of riding and much skill in management of their horses. During the race Miss Simeral was thrown from her horse and badly hurt. Miss Kennedy won the first premium.

The fair continued on these grounds until 1889. The fair in Harrison county was always considered one of the best in the State. It was a great benefit to the farmers. It marks an era in the history of our agricultural advancement. It brought together the farmers, who, having a common interest, studied together by comparison the different kinds

HARRISON COUNTY INFIRMARY.

of stock and farm implements. The fair was moved
to the grounds of Walter Craig in 1889. These
grounds are beautiful. They contain 40 acres taste-
fully studded with young shade trees and enclosed
by a tight' fence. The buildings in the enclosure
are permanent and capacious, and the track, for a
"half mile go" is the best in the State. The following persons have been presidents of the Harrison
county fair: Ezra Cattell, John Hammond, Eli
Peacock, John C. Jamison, Henry Boyles, James B.
Jamison, Samuel Herron, Andrew Jamison, Samuel
Boggs, Obediah Slemmons, Albert Quigley, W. W.
Jamison, Andrew Smith, C. M. Hogg, Samuel Dickerson.

Other fairs in the county are Connotton Valley
Tri-County Agricultural and Mechanical Associa-
tion, located at Jewett, and the Smyrna fair located
at Smyrna.

The following letter is one written by General
Walter B. Beebe, the first lawyer of Harrison county:

CADIZ, COUNTY OF HARRISON, STATE OF OHIO. |
February 14, 1813. |

HONORED PARENTS:

I take this opportunity to inform you that I am
well and in good spirits. Since I left home I have
become tolerably well acquainted with the science of
traveling. I started from St. Clairsville, (the place
from which I wrote you, on or about the 1st of De-
cember, and took a convenient route through the
middle section of this State, a route of about 500
miles. The more I get acquainted with this part of
the country the better I like it. It is certainly the
best land I ever beheld. Judge Ruggles went with
me to Chillicothe, the seat of government, at which

place the Legislature was then sitting. I got acquainted with Governor Meigs and many of the members, who all appear to be very friendly to young men emigrating to this part of the country. Governor Meigs is a yankee from Middletown, Connecticut. At Chillicothe I was examined by the Judges of the Supreme Court of this State, and admitted to practice as an attorney and counsellor at law in the several courts of record in this State. I found a good many counties in my route which I thought would be good places for an attorney, but was induced to settle in this, the county seat of Harrison county, from the following considerations, to-wit: Notwithstanding this county was set off and organized when I was in Chillicothe, yet it is an old settlement and the settlers are generally rich. The inhabitants of this county and counties adjoining have but few yankee settlers, but settled by Virginians, Pennsylvanians, Germans, Scotch, and Irish, who are more litigious and quarrelsome than the yankees are, and pay their money more freely. There is no lawyer in this county, and I have the assurance of being appointed State's Attorney, which will be worth eighty a year, and will be attended with but little trouble and very little inconvenience to other business, being only barred in criminal prosecution from appearing against the State of Ohio.

This county is so situated that there are five other counties within one day's ride of it, and it is the practice in this State for lawyer's to practice in adjoining counties. It is the healthiest part of the State, and the water is good. These, together with other considerations, have induced me, after having been a bird of voyage for three months, to pitch on this place for my permanent home. This town is about 20 miles from the Ohio River, about 70 miles from Pittsburgh, and 16 miles west of St. Clairsville. It is the shire town of the county, and will soon be a populous town. I think my prospects are as good as a young man can reasonably expect, and I have no fear if I have my health.

I am in a land abounding in very many of the good things of this life. I have seen good pot turkeys weighing 20 pounds, sell for 25 cents, hens and chickens 6 cents. Money is very plenty in this State probably more plentiful than usual, owing to its being near the N. W. Army.

I remain your dutiful son,

WALTER B. BEEBE.

To Capt. Stewart Beebe,
Wilbraham, Hamden Co., Mass.

PHYSICIANS OF THE COUNTY.

PHYSICIANS IN 1845.

Martin Wilson, John McBean, A. G. Osburn, John Pearce, George Lucy, Thomas Rowles, William Mills, Thomas Findley, Dr. Harmon, Moses Kennedy, S. Thompson, Wm. Vanhorn, E. H. McCoy, G. W. Duffield, James Bethel, Robert Gamble, Jesse Hall, Horace Belknap, F. C. Robinson, J. H. Stevenson, Wm. G. Smith, T. C. Conn, R. Patton, Jas. Patton, Samuel Black, James P. Barnes, A. T. McClure, I. G. Parry, E. Conaway, Thos. Crumley.

PHYSICIANS IN 1894.

Cadiz—J. D. Wortman, W. T. Sharp, John S. McBean, J. S. Campbell, W. H. Lemmon, Mrs. M. J. Lyons, Miss Mary Lemmon, S. B. McGavran.
Harrisville—A. B. Wilkin, G. H. Colville, J. Comly.
Hopedale—J. D. West, L. A. Crawford.
New Jefferson—Walter Spence.
Jewett—W. L. England, A. C. Grove.
Scio—J. D. Snyder, G. W. Lyle, T. H. Crook, G. W. Custer.
Bowerston—S. B. McGuire.
Franklin—W. A. Welch, James Stone.
Tippecanoe—B. G. Anderson.
Freeport—J. G. Howell, W. A. Zellers.
Piedmont—W. D. Copeland, D. G. Quinn.
Warfel—John Morgan.
Deersville—John Wallace, Frank James.
Hanover—A. C. Nixon.
Moorefield—J. H. Wherry, E. D. Moore.
New Athens—Charles Cobb, Albert Dickerson, James A. McGrew.

GENERAL DESCRIPTION OF HARRISON COUNTY.

Harrison county is divided into 15 townships Shortcreek, Green, Archer, Cadiz, Nottingham, North, Monroe, Franklin, Washington, Freeport, Moorefield, Athens, Stock, German and Rumley.

Principal towns and villages are New Athens, Bowerston, Cadiz, Connotton, Deersville, Freeport, Franklin, Georgetown, Hanover, Harrisville, Hopedale, Moorefield, New Rumley, New Jefferson, Scio, Smyrna and Tippecanoe.

Irregular successions of high hills and deep ravines

occupy the surface but not rough and rocky to such
an extent as to interfere with the agricultural interests of the county. The soil is mostly lime-stone,
and is very productive. Coal and lime-stone abound
in almost inexhaustible quantities. Oil and gas are
found in small quantities at a depth of fourteen hundred feet 1400; in Green and Cadiz Townships.
The land is mostly in a state of cultivation; but a
small per cent. of timber remains. The population
of the county in 1890 was 20,830. Present area in
acres 256,512. The amount of taxes collected in
Harrison county in 1814 was $570.76. The amount
collected in 1893 was $178,056.39. The value of
farm lands, villages and real estate and chattels in
1890 was $13,449,840.

Harrison county is an agricultural county. Our
style of farming will compare favorably with other
counties. Our farmers have adopted all the late improvements in farming implements. Nearly all our
work is done by machinery. We raise in this county
about all the leading kinds of fruit; vegetables of all
kinds can be successfully raised, but the leading one
is the potato, of these we have a number of varieties. Almost all kinds of grain can be raised,
especially wheat and corn. Harrison county is also
a good stock raising county. Our sheep are sought
after in other counties and states, and our wools are
in demand by eastern manufacturers. In fact more
attention is devoted to the raising of sheep than any
other stock. In 1884 the production of wool was 1,-
007,000 lbs.

A great many good horses of different kinds,
are raised in this county, from the fine saddle or
driving horse, to the heavy draft horse

This county is also good as a cattle growing
county. We have several herds of thorough-bred

FARMERS AND MECHANICS NATIONAL BANK.

Shorthorns, Jerseys and Holsteins. Some good hogs are raised, the varieties being Berkshires, Chester Whites and Poland Chinas.

The farms of Harrison county are generally in a good state of cultivation and well improved. Farms sell from $50 to $125 per acre according to quality, improvements and location. There is no better county in Ohio than old Harrison, energetic toil and enterprise characterize her citizens. Her sons and daughters are to be found in almost every State and engaged in all manner of honorable avocations, and wherever they are they do their duty cheerfully and bravely, and retain in their hearts a lingering affection for the hills and valleys among which they were nurtured.

SCRAPS OF HISTORY.

E. M. Stanton whose wonderful executive capacity as head of the War Department has given him renown throughout all the world, was at one time an active member of the Cadiz bar and the third Prosecuting Attorney of Harrison county.

Cadiz Branch of the P. C. C. & St. L. R. R. was opened to Cadiz on the 11th of June, 1854.

Messrs. Biggs and Beatty laid out the town of Cadiz in 1804.

New Rumley was laid out August 15, 1814; Freeport in 1814; New Athens in 1817; Deersville in 1815; Harrisville in 1817.

Magdalena Grundy is said to be the first white woman to cross the Connotton creek west, and loca-

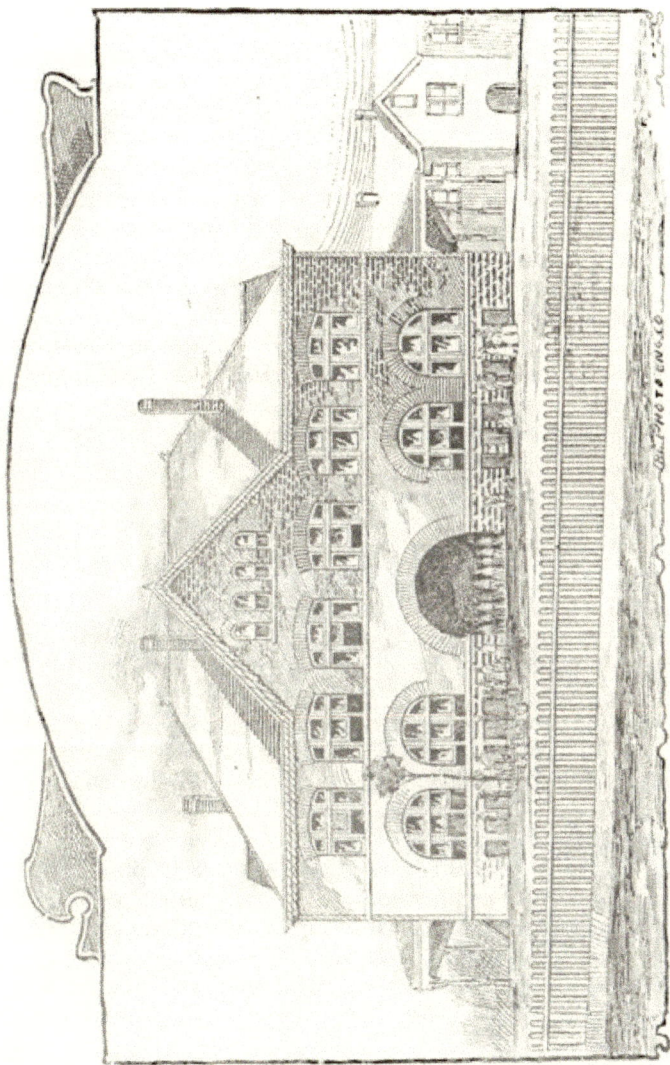

HARRISON COUNTY CHILDREN'S HOME.

ted with her husband on the farm well-known as the
John M. Holmes' farm near the village of Connotton.

Dr. T. R. Crawford was pastor of the Nottingham Presbyterian church for 40 years.

April 29, 1866, the Harrison National Bank, of
Cadiz, was robbed of about $260,000. Within a few
days the burglars were captured, and most of the
money found in their possession.

William Duvall has been a faithful and obliging
conductor on the Cadiz Branch for 27 years.

Dr. William Custer, of Scio, Dr. William Beadle,
of Green township, Dr. John McBean, of Cadiz, and
Dr. R. H. Simmons, of Deersville, were regarded in
their day as the leading physicians of the county.

John A. Bingham was elected in 1854 as a Representative to the XXXIV Congress from the Twenty-
first Ohio District, and was a member of every Congress from the Twenty-first and Sixteenth Ohio districts except the XXXVIII, until March 4, 1873.
In May, 1873, Mr. Bingham was appointed by President Grant Envoy Extraordinary and Minister
Plenipotentiary to Japan, which position he held for
twelve years.

Without detracting from the deserts of others, it
might be said that H. S. McFadden in his day, did
more extensive general trade than any other man in
the history of Harrison county.

Matthew Simpson D. D., L. L. D., was born in
Cadiz, June 20, 1811, and died in Philadelphia, Pa.,
June 18, 1884. He was one of the most eminent
preachers in the Methodist Episcopal Church. He
was elected a bishop in 1852.

Gen. George A. Custer, the famed cavalry leader
of the War of the Rebellion, was born in New Rumley, Dec. 5, 1839.

Stewart Price was the first merchant, the first

postmaster, and the first railroad agent at the town of
Bowerston.

Capt. H. B. Heller, of Monroe township, during
his life took an active interest in the advancement and
improvement of Harrison county, and his public
spirit manifested itself in many ways.

Mrs. Nancy Dewey, widow of Hon. Chauncey
Dewey, was born near Uniontown, Pa., October 27,
1804. In 1807 her parents located on a wild piece of
land near Cadiz, which at that time contained but
few houses and around which the wolves, panthers,
and other wild animals of the early days were still
plentiful. The Indians were also numerous, and would
come in parties to trade with the white pioneers,
bringing with them many beautifully worked articles
such as moccasins ornamented with colored beads and
porcupine quills, and belts made of snakes skins, all
painted and woven together and profusely decorated
with beads. The squaws would have their pappooses
strapped on boards and carried on their backs, and
when tired would stand pappoose, board and all
against some convenient tree. The Indians used to
bring baskets in for trade in large quantities, tied
about their bodies in such numbers that it was difficult to decide whether Indian or baskets walked.
Mrs. Dewey has a vivid recollection of the pioneer
days. She still resides in Cadiz and is a noble woman.

Julius Schreiber, was pre-eminently one of the
pioneers and promoters of the business interests of
Harrison county, although not, strictly speaking, one
of the early settlers.

John N. Haverfield was born in Cadiz township,
May 17, 1820, and died at his residence in Stock
township, April 10, 1894. Mr. Haverfield was a
leading farmer and one of the best men in Harrison
county.

June 6, 1823, the commissioners of the county fixed a rate for wolf scalps in addition to that allowed by the State. For all wolf scalps above the age of six months $1.50; on all scalps under six months 75 cents.

The first couple married in Harrison county were Lakin Wells and Cynthia Maffett, on February 4, 1813, the ceremony being performed by Andrew McNeely, Justice of the Peace.

Wm. H. Lucas has been a teacher in the Cadiz Schools for twenty-one years.

We omitted to mention the name of H. S. Black, of Freeport, in our list of physicians of 1894.

The following were the first directors in the First National Bank: John Hammond, John Green, Isaac Thomas, Marshall McCall, Robert Pittis, John Carnahan, Samuel Slemmons, Samuel George, Joseph S. Thomas.

The Associate Reformed Church, mention of which is made in our article on Courts, as the building in which the first courts of Harrison county were held, was a log building, erected on grounds purchased from Zachariah Biggs, situated on the corner of South and Ohio streets. The log building was torn down and a substantial brick building erected in the year 1828.

The oldest male resident of Cadiz is Mr. Benjamin Timmons, who has resided on the ground upon which he now lives for 81 years. Mrs. Agnes Mealy is the oldest woman now living in Cadiz, having passed her ninetieth milestone in life's journey on October 17, 1893. May they, with all our old people, live many more years among us.

The grand and great-grand-children of the contractor of the court house built in 1815, are living in Cadiz.

Mrs. Christina Kimmel, who resides one-half mile

north of Jewett, reached her 100th birthday on
March 7, 1894, the oldest woman in the county. Mrs.
Kimmel had been living 21 years before the court
house recently torn down was erected.

REMINISCENCES OF MORGAN'S RAID
THROUGH MOOREFIELD.

On a bright and beautiful day in July, 1863, the
peace and quiet of our little village was disturbed by
the anticipated invasion of Rebel forces numbering
five or six hundred mounted cavalry, under command
of the noted Rebel General John Morgan. The air
was full of rumors of the great destruction of property along the line of march, and the alarm for the
safety of family and property became intense. This
feeling of insecurity was somewhat increased when
M. J. Brown and John Robinson, of Cadiz, driving
a spirited team, rushed through here to discover if
possible the line of march the Rebels were likely to
take. In about an hour, or perhaps less, they returned, furiously driving Jehu like, announcing that
the Rebels were coming this way, and would be with
us in a short time.

Very soon thereafter we discovered the bridge over
Big Stillwater on fire, and a few minutes later, another smoke, looming up about one-half mile east,
indicated that the other covered bridge over Little
Stillwater (or Boggs' Fork) was also being consumed.

About this time many laughable incidents occurred
that did not seem so funny at the time; men hiding

their valuables in the most unthought of places, secreting their horses in thickets and deep hollows; women and children running hither and thither with their trinkets trying to find some very secure place to hide them, being so excited as to forget where they placed them, and had to be reminded by their neighbors who chanced to observe where they put them, where to look for them. A few would-be Generals on horseback, were riding our village street, giving spicy directions as to what others should do, or where to go. A thing they soon found out when the advance guard of Morgan's force came galloping into town, putting them to flight, and quite an exciting race occurred through our street accompanied with the Rebel yell, "Halt, Halt!" Some were immediately captured and their horses taken; others didn't have time to obey orders, and got away, doing some exceedingly fast riding to accomplish the feat. Very soon after this race the main force entered our town and took complete possession of the streets, stables, and every house that had been vacated by the occupants, not disturbing or forcibly entering any house where families remained at home. They seemed to be a hungry set, and freely solicited every house for provisions of every description; some of them exhibiting abnormal appetites for pound cake and preserves. After cleaning up all the previously prepared provisions in the town they quietly sought rest and sleep, seemingly as unconcerned as though the Union forces in pursuit were a hundred miles back instead of three or four. Morgan himself occupied the parlor bed at the Mills' Hotel, and seemed to be taking a refreshing sleep, while his body guard, with their revolvers lying upon chairs at their sides, or on the bed where Morgan was sleeping, occupied the time in reading the news, with which

they seemed to be well provided. When Morgan
arose from the bed he walked to the front door,
stepped out upon the pavement, cast his eye down the
street, then turned and walked leisurely up street
unattended; later the order was given to mount, and
their march eastward continued, taking the road to
New Athens, accompanied by escorts drafted into
service as guides across the country.' The Union
forces under command of Shackelford, having been
delayed by reason of the destroyed bridges, did not
get into town in full force until after night,
when hungry soldiers had again to be fed, and right
nobly did our women work cooking and serving food
until after midnight. A greater number of the
Union forces pushed on after Morgan, but a portion
remained over night, probably as a reminder to us
that the war was still going on. Stragglers continued coming into town the following day, but by evening quiet again reigned supreme, and the war was
over, so far as our town's actual experience was con-
cerned.

1813   1894.

"We leap the chasm of 81 years. Span the dis-
tance between the historic then and the eventful
now. We regard Pioneer days in Harrison county,
as a thing of the past. The wilderness has been
changed into the cultivated field; the log cabin to
the mansion. The hominy block to the mill with
its improvements. The lone track through the forests to good roads, to the iron rail, fastmail and
electric wire with its lightning messenger. The
wolf, bear and deer have disappeared, their places
being occupied by the more docile and useful animals
of the cultivated field. New systems of tillage and

new devisements of agriculture have been introduced, a thorough change has overtaken the farm and the utensils of the farm. Instead of the cheery blaze of the glowing pine we have the dazzling chandelier, the gas and electric lights. In our honors name, however, let it be recorded that we are not an ungrateful posterity. May the memories of our pioneer fathers long be cherished, and their names be held in admiring esteem and reverence. May no ungrateful thought be entertained or unkind or rude word be spoken to the few who survive and patiently wait for the white wave to lift them free. The shore, the palm, the victory, the rest is but yonder.

> " Another land more bright than this,
> To their dim sight appears,
> And on their way to it they'll soon
> Again be pioneers."

When it becomes necessary to build another Temple of Justice for Harrison County, aside from any accident will the generation then living call us pioneers?"

CONTENTS.

INDEX TO ILLUSTRATIONS.